D1492638

Ann Summers little book of kama sutra

EBURY
PRESS

First published in Great Britain in 2008

3 5 7 9 10 8 6 4 2

Text written by Siobhan Kelly © Ebury Press 2008
Photographs © John Freeman 2008

Addresses for companies within the Random House Group can be
found at www.randomhouse.co.uk

A CIP catalogue record for this book is available from the British
Library

Art direction and design by Smith & Gilmour, London
Photography by John Freeman

ISBN: 9780091916442

The Random House Group Limited makes every effort to ensure
that the papers used in our books are made from trees that have
been legally sourced from well-managed and credibly certified
forests. Our paper procurement policy can be found on www.
randomhouse.co.uk

Printed and bound in Singapore by Tien Wah Press Ltd

To buy books by your favourite authors and register for offers visit
www.rbooks.co.uk

Foreword

Welcome to Ann Summers' fun, fresh version of the world's oldest and most famous sex manual, the Kama Sutra. This 2,000-year-old mystical sex guide contains the secrets of the sex you've always wished you could have. We've given you a 21st-century take on sex secrets that have been satisfying lovers all over the world for over two millennia. These pages could contain the key to a new, deeper, more intense kind of sex. Experiment and enjoy.

Jacqueline Gold
Chief Executive, Ann Summers

Contents

The Kama Sutra

Browse any sex shop and you'll be astonished at the range of bold, brilliant books that can help you enhance your lovemaking. There are books about straight sex, gay sex, kinky sex, vanilla sex, sex with toys, safe sex, sex with strangers and sex with spouses. And all of them draw inspiration from the world's first sex manual. The Kama Sutra, written by an Indian prince in 4,000 BC, is the original guide to great sex. And we can still learn a lot from it today.

True, the world has changed a lot in the 2,400 years since the Kama Sutra was first published. Attitudes towards sex, health and religion have changed. Mankind has had a million adventures and made some stunning advances. But there's still one experience we've never managed to surpass. The thrill of getting naked and making love with another human being still remains the most intense, exciting and potentially rewarding experience we can have. Bodies still become as passionately aroused as they ever did. Hearts still fall as passionately in love. Orgasm is still as delicious.

So what is the Kama Sutra? It's popularly known as a collection of exotically bendy sex positions that require the strength and flexibility of an Olympic gymnast to master. And it's true that some positions the book describes do resemble a particularly ambitious game of Twister.

But there's more to the Kama Sutra than simply a variety of sex positions. It's based on an ancient Indian belief that sex is a way of reaching spiritual awareness, worshipping

The Kama Sutra says that sex can sometimes give us a glimpse of heaven.

the gods and cleansing the soul. In Hindu thought, sex is not only considered natural and necessary but also sacred, mimicking the creation of the world.

The Kama Sutra covers all aspects of sex, from seduction and conversation, through to meditation, foreplay, oral sex and masturbation, love potions and even primitive sex toys.

Who, what and when?

In 400 BC, an elderly Indian sage called Mallinaga Vatsyayana set down a series of sutras or sayings about love. We don't know much about his life, but it seemed that he took it upon himself to gather together ancient Hindu legends – such as the story of god and goddess Shiva and Parvati who made love in their bedroom in a palace for 10,000 years – and instructions for the art of marriage. The manual was written primarily for young, urban men discovering sex for the first time. Women reap the benefits of this wisdom, as Vatsyayana stresses the importance of putting the woman's orgasm first. He states that women, being tender creatures, want 'tender beginnings', introducing the concept for foreplay long before glossy women's magazines explained it to us in the 1960s!

Using many of the same principles as yoga, the Kama Sutra emphasises breathing in time with your partner and making a spiritual connection rather than the fast, furious thrusting of more conventional Western sex. The techniques are designed to delay the man's orgasm (and so conserve the sexual energy ancient Indians valued so highly) and intensify the female orgasm.

The original Kama Sutra was written for men, but in our version, all instructions are unisex, to reflect the equality of modern relationships.

part one

tender beginnings

While the Kama Sutra is known around the world for its list of positions, there is more to the art of love making Kama Sutra-style, which is what this part of the book is concerned with. From understanding his and her sex zones to learning seduction and deep breathing techniques, these pages can only add to the excitements contained in part two.

Ancient wisdom for modern lovers

So what relevance does this dusty old book have today? The Kama Sutra can offer an antidote to the fast-paced, super-sexed society we live in today. It offers us a way to explore all aspects of our sexuality – to stimulate all our senses and tap into the softer, more spiritual side of sex that 21st-century Westerners tend to think of sex as a bodily function, a route to orgasm, and while this is true, there's so much more to sex than that. Many of us yearn for something simpler and more natural but don't know how to go about bringing tenderness and spirituality back into the bedroom.

Ancient Indian wisdom says that a couple who follow the Kama Sutra will remain faithful to each other for 100 years.

Tantric sex

Tantric sex made headlines a few years ago as a celebrity sex trend that involved making love for hours on end. It's true that advanced tantric practitioners with years of experience can experience massively extended sex sessions, but that's only part of it.

Both tantric sex and the Kama Sutra offer a different, more spiritual way of looking at sex. The Kama Sutra uses many of the principles of tantric sex – but they're not quite the same thing.

The Kama Sutra is easy to summarise – it's a written set of rules designed to enhance lovemaking. Tantric sex itself is a vague concept and one that's hard to pin down. Tantra literally translates as 'the way' and basically sees sex as worship. Although it's based on ancient Hindu and Bhuddist techniques, it's wisdom that has been passed down through the generations – we don't know of any surviving document that sums it up.

As well as the Kama Sutra, two other ancient Asian sex books were written – The Ananga Ranga and The Perfumed Garden. Some wisdom from those books is incorporated into these pages.

Tantra is about energy and spirituality: the emphasis is on lovers whose minds meet long before their bodies come together, and focuses on meditation and closeness. Penetrative sex will be a natural consequence of achieving spiritual unity. In tantric sex, partners are encouraged to explore the opposite aspects of their nature. So the woman can take a dynamic role while her partner relinquishes control and relaxes into his softer, more feminine side.

Tantric practitioners also believe that every time a man ejaculates he loses vital, sacred energy so the aim of tantric sex is to avoid the male orgasm for as long as possible – good news for women who usually take longer to climax than men. For tantric tips that help to delay ejaculation, see page 25.

It's a discipline that takes years to truly master, but try the meditation exercises in this book for a tantric taster – it could be the beginning of a whole new adventure for you and your lover.

Kiss and make up, Kama-Sutra style: 'When fury separates a couple, they should calm each other with affectionate words and embraces so they may come together again in desire.'

The sacred body

Think you know your way around your body? Think again. There's more to your sex zones than the basic biology we're taught in sex ed. In the Kama Sutra, male and female sex organs represent much more than just sources of physical pleasure. They are sacred representations of the divine male and female energy that creates life.

Re-thinking your attitude to your body is a vital step to truly mastering the principles of the Kama Sutra. Oh, and once you've experienced foreplay and oral sex Kama Sutra-style, you'll never look back.

Her sex zone – the yoni

In Hindu culture the vagina is known as the yoni and is associated with the goddess Shakti, the divine female energy source. It is the source of creation, so it is held in admiration, awe and respect. Ancient Indians believed that like a mouth, it swallowed up and consumed the male seed.

Looking at your yoni in a mirror is the best way to identify the different zones, each of which are sensitive in their own way.

- ❀ The vulva is the fleshy entrance to the vagina – the bit you can see when you take your panties off.
- ❀ The vagina is the inside bit that you can't see. When a woman is turned on, it swells up with blood and produces natural lubrication to help ease the penis in. The bottom one-third of the vagina is the most sensitive; the further up the vagina you go, the less the nerve endings can be stimulated.

- The clitoris is a tiny bud of flesh nestled under a hood of skin at the top of the vulva, near where you pee. Stroking, licking and caressing it is the most sure-fire way of bringing a woman to orgasm.

- The G-spot is a highly erogenous zone located about 5cm up the front wall of the vagina. This mass of nerve tissue can't be felt unless it's stimulated, whether that's by a finger, a penis or a sex toy, and it's said to be the size of a baked bean. It's highly controversial – many women say that stimulation on the front of the vaginal wall does absolutely nothing for them, while others report massively strong orgasms.

  The Kama Sutra makes no mention of the G-spot, which wasn't identified by scientists until the 20th century, but many of the positions in the book, especially those that involve penetration from behind, seem custom-made to give G-spot orgasms.

Ancient Indian art represents the yoni as a downward-pointing triangle. A man who uses his tongue to trace tiny triangles on his lover's clitoris will find that his 'worship' is gratefully received.

His sex zone – the lingam

You don't have to go too far in Hindu art to find recreations of the erect penis, or lingam, as the male sex organ is known in the Kama Sutra. It was the representation of Shiva, the dominant male God, and was worshipped by all.

Although most men have been playing with their penises since they were tiny boys, a detailed examination of the lingam can inspire you to experiment with the way you touch yourself – and the way your lover touches you.

- ❀ The 'stalk' of the penis is known as the shaft. The first 5–7.5cm are the most sensitive.
- ❀ The tip, or head, is the most nerve-packed area of the male body. Sometimes it's covered by a foreskin (a protective layer of loose skin that peels back when a man is aroused). If he's circumcised, the foreskin will be removed and the head will be exposed.
- ❀ The testicles hang loosely behind the penis in a little sack of skin called the scrotum.
- ❀ The prostate gland, located a couple of centimetres up the front wall of the rectum, is often referred to as the male equivalent of the G-spot. The prostate gland is *incredibly* sensitive to pressure. Some men enjoy a little anal stimulation with toys, tongues or fingers.
- ❀ For men who don't like backdoor action, the perineum – the area of skin between the balls and anus – is also sensitive to pressure and it's a way of accessing the prostate gland without penetrating the anus.

Representations of the lingam are in Indian temples even today. Worship your man's lingam – there isn't a man alive who doesn't adore hearing his lover vocally praise his erection.

Little Women and Mr Big – a word on size

In the Kama Sutra, men and women were each put into three categories depending on the size of their yoni or lingam. A man could be a hare (small), bull (bigger) or a stallion (biggest). Women on the other hand, were known as deer (small), mare (bigger) or elephant (biggest). Vatsyayana strongly recommends that the most satisfying unions are those that take place between matched types – deer woman with hare man, mare woman with bull man, elephant woman with stallion man.

Today, we're aware that most penises are compatible with most vaginas – in fact, the yoni and the lingam who can't achieve a happy union are rare creatures indeed. But if there's a huge discrepancy in your sizes, try this:

❀ If his large penis makes sex uncomfortable, try positions where the vagina is lengthened and penetration is shallow, like The Twining (page 63).
❀ If his penis feels small, try rear-entry positions, or those where the angle of the legs shortens the vagina, like The Cats (page 88).

Masturbation, Kama Sutra-style

For much of the 20th century, there was an unhealthy attitude to solo sex, or masturbation – where you use your hand, or a toy, to reach a climax. Everybody was doing it, but nobody was talking about it. It was assumed that men were all masturbating like mad, but many people felt that it was improper – abnormal, even – for women to touch themselves for sexual pleasure.

Thankfully, the Kama Sutra has no time for that kind of nonsense. The truth is, it's vital for both sexes to touch themselves for pleasure as well as to enjoy caresses within the partnership. How can you tell your partner what you like if you've never experimented yourself? And the ancient text is full of techniques that show both men and woman how to get the most out of sex – whether there's someone else in the room or not.

Ladies first – masturbation for women

Various techniques for rubbing the yoni were recommended in the Kama Sutra. It was considered important for a woman to 'unlock' all the creative life-giving sexual energy trapped in her yoni. It was considered important for a woman's wellbeing, both mental and spiritual as well as bodily, to unleash this energy from time to time. The Kama Sutra also emphasised the importance of a woman knowing how to arouse herself so that she can show her partner what she likes, and get herself ready to accept his penis.

If you've never masturbated before, take some time to explore your body. Find a place where you are comfortable and won't be disturbed. Breathe deeply (see exercises on pages 32–33) to release tension and let go of the day's stresses.

Masturbation is about your mind as well as your body, so read an erotic novel or watch your favourite love scene from a film, fantasise about your partner or even download or rent an erotic movie. Buy some lubricant from a sex shop so that you can supplement your natural juices.

With your two forefingers, gently stroke your clitoris and trail your fingers over your labia. To begin with, keep up a steady rhythm, lots of fluttering little strokes. Once you learn what gets you off, you can experiment and eke out your pleasure by teasing your body with lots of little stop-start movements. The key is to keep up a slow, steady rhythm on your clit: it takes the average woman 20 minutes to reach orgasm, and if you've never climaxed before, it can take longer still.

Experiment with positions:

- 🏵 If you don't get anywhere lying on your back, turn over and lie on your front, with your hands underneath your pelvis: the extra weight of your body on your hand can provide the additional friction it takes.

- 🏵 If your clit is too sensitive for the direct touch of your fingers, or you prefer the feeling of being touched by something else, try rubbing against your pillow – the clit looks like a tiny bud of flesh, but the nerve endings fan out throughout your pelvic area, so direct stimulation isn't always the most effective way to reach orgasm.

- 🏵 If you get frustrated because nothing's happening, do your deep breathing exercises, read your rude book and start again. The whole point with tantric sex is to explore your mind, body and spirit rather than achieve orgasm, so don't put undue pressure on yourself. If it doesn't work tonight, try again tomorrow. The important thing is that whatever you're doing feels good and right for you.

❀ If touching yourself doesn't get you off – or you just fancy a change – use a vibrator on a low setting held against your clit, or even clamped between your knees (first-time sex-toy users are often unprepared for the speed and strength of modern vibrators and end up bruising or numbing the very parts they're trying to stimulate).

You're more likely to climax with a toy than with your hands alone. Once you've had one orgasm, your body knows the fabulous high it's chasing, and you're more likely to give yourself another one. Do keep experimenting with your hands, as toys can be just a little bit addictive …

Give that man a hand – male masturbation

Most men have so much practice when it comes to masturbation that they think there is nothing more they could possibly learn. Not true! Mastering the Kama Sutra involves un-learning the solo-sex techniques you've been using all your life, and viewing masturbation in a completely different light. Most guys grow up masturbating quickly for fear of being caught, and can climax in a few seconds. But much of the Kama Sutra is about the man prolonging his pleasure until she's had hers. The good news is, there are techniques that you can use to train yourself to last longer.

First of all, change your usual position. If you usually masturbate lying or sitting down, try kneeling. This will make the blood rush to a different part of your body away from your penis. If you usually use pornography, try letting your imagination provide the pictures. As you touch yourself, avoid the temptation to use firm, hard strokes and make them light and soft.

This alone will buy you more time.

Typically, your breathing becomes faster and shallower as you come near to climax. It's a natural reflex, and one you've probably never thought about challenging. But by controlling something as simple as your breathing patterns by basing them on yoga techniques, you can learn to control, delay or even avoid ejaculation.

As you feel you're about to come – but before you've reached that point of no return where nothing on earth could prevent your orgasm – stop touching yourself and focus on your breathing. Count slowly to four as you inhale, and slowly to four as you exhale. Don't touch your dick again until you feel your erection begin to subside. Keep this up for as long as you can bear to, and with practice you can treble the length of time it takes for you to come. This technique can be interpreted into intercourse or foreplay by withdrawing from your partner and concentrating on her pleasure for a few moments before returning to your penis.

Once you've mastered this, try 'dry coming', developed by ancient Indians as it was thought taboo for a man to 'waste his seed', regarded as a precious, life-giving energy.

Masturbate as above, but when you stop touching yourself, squeeze your pubococcygeus (PC) muscle, which encircles the base of the penis and the anus (it's the one you use to stop and start the flow when you're peeing). Instead of thinking about your semen spurting out, visualise it turning back in on itself, travelling back down the penis, up the spine and dispersing through your body.

Men who successfully complete this exercise say they come but they don't ejaculate and they have full-body orgasms that can be felt for hours afterwards. And when you fill your own body with that energy, you have conserved it all. This can also be used during intercourse, but not as a method of safe sex or birth control – even the most advanced tantra practitioners lose control sometimes!

Exotic playthings

Think sex toys are relatively new? Think again! The Kama Sutra states that the 'women of the royal harem' (these would have been courtesans and the most sexually skilled women of their time) would often pleasure themselves with 'bulbs, roots and fruits having the form of the lingam'.

Luckily, you don't have to raid the greengrocers for interestingly shaped root vegetables. It's much easier and more hygienic to use a specially-made dildo –a fake penis, usually made of rubber or plastic, available in variety of sizes in sex shops – to experiment with the kind of size, pressure and thrusting you like. Sliding a dildo into your pussy while you stroke your clitoris is a great way to enjoy the feeling of penetration and stimulation simultaneously. Vibrators, too, are a great way to achieve the clitoral stimulation that most women feel is vital to orgasm.

And ancient sex toys weren't just for women. The Kama Sutra refers to apadrayvas, objects that are put on or around the penis to supplement its length or thickness. Their 21st-century equivalent are cock rings, which are designed to fit around the base of the penis and the scrotum, restricting flow out of the penis. This can be useful for prolonging an erection until the woman's pleasure has been taken care of. A cock ring stops the balls rising up into your body, which happens at the point of orgasm – so stops the orgasm until you remove the ring. They can be made from stretchy rubber or metal, silicone or leather, and are also available in sex shops. Never wear it for longer than 20 minutes, and take it off right away if it starts to hurt. Avoid if you have blood pressure problems or clots or diabetes.

Chakras

Tantric sex uses chakras to map out the body. According to this philosophy, there are seven different points on the body, which are the centres for different kinds of energies. Each chakra has its own colour and is associated with a certain spiritual, physical and emotional state.

During lovemaking, use any one of these chakras as an erogenous zone. For example, if you're having problems with self-confidence, then ask your love to kiss and caress your solar plexus chakra – the manipura. Focusing on chakras during solo meditation can also help clear blocked energies. See page 36 for a chakra meditation you can do together before sex.

Sahasrara (Violet)
Crown chakra – is the centre of spiritual connection and ecstasy. Just above the crown of the head

Ajna (Purple)
The brow chakra, also known as the 'third eye', is imagination and perception.
Between the eyes

Vishudda (Blue)
The throat chakra relates to self-knowledge and expression.
On the neck

Anahata (Green)
The heart chakra is the centre of love, sharing and trust.
Between the nipples

Manipura (Yellow)
The solar plexus chakra is the centre of confidence.
At the bottom of the rib cage

Svadhishtana (Orange)
The sacral chakra is the centre of balance, movement and stability.
Just below the navel

Muladhara (Red)
The base chakra is the centre of sexual desire and childbirth.
In the pelvis

The Kama Sutra way of foreplay

Although it's famous for its positions, the Kama Sutra places as much – if not more – emphasis on preparing for sex than on the act itself. In Vatsyayana's time, it was assumed that couples would not have had sex before their wedding night, and he suggested men court their partners for ten days after marriage. You don't have to hold out for ten days – but finding harmony together before you go to bed can take sex to a whole new level.

Seduction scenes

The room where you have sex is important. The Kama Sutra recommends 'a pleasure room, decorated with flowers and fragrant with perfume'. If your budget doesn't stretch to dozens of rose petals, then you can at least make sure that your bed linen is fresh, crisp and welcoming. It's a good idea to prioritise your bedroom as somewhere that's just for sex and sleeping – try to clear your room of televisions, radios and other distractions.

The Kama Sutra also advises that you should spend ten days talking and 'playing and singing'. Again, it's not necessary for you to learn the sitar and serenade your lover every night. What is important is that you make time to talk, caress, perhaps eat and drink, but always stop short of penetrative sex. Take this time to experiment and find out each other's turn-ons. Read erotic literature aloud to each other. Present each other with gifts – sex toys, body paint, lube – anything that gives your lover a clue as to the kind of sex you'd like at the end of your 'courtship'.

Undressing each other was a key part of the Kama Sutra lovemaking ritual: either undress each other or perform a slow, sexy striptease. Wear lots of fine layers and strip down to your best, freshest underwear – there's no need to get totally naked if you don't want to.

Bathing and anointing the body, too, were essential aspects of Kama Sutra foreplay that can greatly enhance sex for modern lovers. As well as ensuring your bodies are clean and fresh and pleasant, which shows basic respect, the nurturing practice of washing each other in the bath or shower and massaging oil into each other's bodies is perfect for getting into the soft, spiritual zone that Kama Sutra love-making is all about. Touching and caressing here should still be done with tenderness rather than outright sexuality. Adorn each other's bodies – he could slowly do up the bow on a pair of tie-side panties, she could lovingly help him fasten a chain around his neck.

Agree not to have sex for a few nights. The longer you leave it, the deeper your spiritual bonds will be – and the stronger your orgasms when you do have sex.

A word on tantric breathing techniques

Breathing is the essence of life – even we in the West know that! But while we see it as a basic biological function, Eastern wisdom has always viewed it as prana, an important connection between the body and the soul. The flow of breath through the body is thought to represent the flow of life and so is endowed with power and energy.

Learning to charge the body with energy through deep breathing will clear your mind ready for sex. Breathing techniques increase intimacy between partners at any stage. Focusing on your breathing helps to centre you and makes you fully conscious of the moment and not distracted by everyday thoughts like your shopping list or work worries. Taking deep breaths also helps to relax your entire body and produces a feeling of calm and wellbeing that seems to rise up from your very core. On a basic biological level, it will get oxygen flowing all over your body so that when you finally touch each other, your skin and nerve endings will be highly sensitised.

Inhale, exhale Many different breathing and visualisation techniques can be used to help link your energy with your partner's, but first of all you need to learn to control your breathing on your own. Find a peaceful space where you won't be disturbed. Lie down on your back, on a bed or on a mat on the floor, whichever is most comfortable for you.

❀ Close your eyes.
❀ Think about each body part in turn, beginning with your toes and working up through your legs, pelvis and upper body. Imagine that each breath revives and feeds it.
❀ Keep breathing, but now inhale and exhale as slowly and deeply as you can. Breathe from your belly and not from your chest – short, shallow breathing could make you dizzy. Think about the air going in and out and how your skin feels. Whenever your attention wanders to the niggles of everyday life, return to the awareness of your breathing and nothing else.

Holding your breath just before the moment of climax can make the experience even more intense.

Basic breathing meditation for two Sit close facing and stare deep into each other's eyes. Feel as if you are looking into the middle of your lover's soul: picturing a lotus flower between your partner's nipples, on the heart chakra, can help you to focus your attention. Then close your eyes, breathe slow and deep, focusing on nothing but your inhalation and exhalation.

❀ Let your breath begin to move in time with your lover's. You should naturally fall into a pattern together, like the rise and fall of a wave.

❀ If you find it hard to synchronise breathing patterns, one of you can lead while the other follows. Once you're breathing together, reverse this so that the other partner takes the lead, and alternate 'leaders' until you naturally breathe together.

Caressing meditation

You will both get a turn at this, so either partner can go first. Begin with a breathing meditation for two to synchronise your energies. One partner lies back on the bed, eyes closed, while the active partner gently caresses him or her from head to toe. Use the three middle fingers and concentrate on every inch of the body apart from the genitals. Keep stroking and caressing for 20 minutes. While you're caressing your partner, visualise him or her as a god or prince, goddess or princess, and think of your caresses as a gift of worship. If your mind wanders, focus on breathing together.

The meditation of the five senses This is a real treat for when one of you wants to pamper the other and entice him or her into sex. Start with your basic breathing meditation. Then the passive partner lies back while the other partner blindfolds him or her, and prepares to pamper and lavish attention by indulging each of the five senses in turn.

- ❁ **Smell** – rub an essential oil or a fragranced massage oil on his chest.
- ❁ **Sound** – whisper words of love and sexy things you'd like to try in his ear.
- ❁ **Taste** – slick your lips with flavoured lube and kiss your partner.
- ❁ **Touch** – trail a feather over his body and watch him shiver.
- ❁ **Sight** – take off the blindfold and allow your lover to drink in the sight of your naked body.

Chakra meditation This is an advanced tantric meditation, so make sure you're confident with your ability to concentrate and breathe together for extended periods before you try it. Sit facing away from each other, your legs crossed and your backs touching, hands in your laps with your palms facing upwards. Breathe deeply for five minutes, coordinating, feel your lungs expand and collapse together. Then begin to focus on each chakra in turn (have this book open at page 28 if you don't want to memorise them all!).

- Start with muladhara , the base chakra, which is in your pelvis. Focus on that part of your body and think about the emotions and energies associated with this energy centre – sexual pleasure, reproduction.
- Visualise the rich reds of the chakra. Let the colour flood your mind until your inner eye sees nothing else but a sea of colour.
- Repeat the same process for each chakra, spending three minutes (or as long as it feels good) for each one. When your meditation is over, spend five minutes breathing. From there, you can turn to face each other and move into a kissing position.

37

It takes time to master these meditations. If you fund your attention begins to wander, revert to the basic breathing meditation on page 34 for as long as it takes you to feel close again.

Kama's kisses

A wonderful kiss is a pleasure in its own right as well as great foreplay. Vatsyayana wrote that a man should kiss his lover gently and gracefully on the mouth and that this is the key to 'unlocking her passion and desire', and he wasn't wrong. Some people even report that an intense kiss can trigger orgasm.

The Kama Sutra says you must keep your mouth tidy, sweet and clean. It's about respect and consideration – after all, you want your lover to kiss you back. So floss, brush, gargle and get ready for kissing like you've never experienced.

The nominal kiss This is a tentative, try kiss. Lovers gently touch each other's lips but nothing else, getting used to the feel of each other's mouths, breathing in time and savouring the energy that flows between them.

The pressed kiss One partner firmly presses against the other's lower lip, either with her lips or a finger. This pressure, especially when done by the finger and accompanied by full lip contact, moves things on a stage.

The turned kiss One partner takes the other's chin or face in hand and turns it upwards. It exposes the lips and mouth for full exploration.

The upper lip kiss Known in Sanskrit as uttarachumbita, the kiss of the upper lip is a Kama classic. Using his tongue and lower lip, the man gently sucks on the woman's top lip, while she in turn kisses his lower lip. He pays particular attention to where the upper lip meets the gum. Tantric teaching says that the nerves here are directly linked to the clitoris.

The clasping kiss One partner clasps or presses the other's lips between her own lips, creating erotic pressure. From here, gently explore each other's mouths with your tongues.

Kama Sutra kissing games

Sex is one of the few areas where adults are allowed to get playful, and the Kama Sutra acknowledged this. The book describes a game where each lover tries to be the first to catch their partner's lips between the teeth.

If the woman loses, says Vatsyayana, 'she should pretend to cry, and turn away from him'. Then she should wait until he's asleep, then 'get hold of his lower lip and hold it in her teeth, so that he should not slip away'. She should celebrate her victory by 'laughing and dancing about'. In modern terms, this fun competition can progress into a pillow fight, or light play-fighting. Or you can make up your own forfeits – the loser having to lavish 20 minutes' massage on the winning partner.

Don't save kisses just for the face! You can explore all zones of your lover's body. Remember that you're worshipping your partner with your mouth – full body kisses can be a great way to do this when words just aren't enough.

Head rush

In the Kama Sutra, the head is one of the most important erogenous zones – it's the closest part of our body to the heavens and worthy of special attention for that reason.

The following techniques were important aspects of foreplay and lovemaking to the ancient Indians – as important as kissing, caressing or oral sex. All tips are unisex.

Two hands in the hair The couple is sitting or standing. He entwines his fingers in the hair at the side of her head, palms against the face, and pulls the two of them together in a passionate kiss. He presses her lower lip, and she responds with the same action.

Drawing and kissing She runs her fingers through the hair at the back of his head and draws the two heads together in a pressing kiss. With the other hand, she strokes his face and neck.

Pull of the dragon Lovers stand with bodies pressing together and legs entwined. He grabs her hair at the back, and they press their mouths together in a deep, tongue kiss. Though sex has not taken place, the couple are united from head to toe.

Embracing hair union You hold each other's hair just above the ears and hold your lover's face close. Look deep into each other's eyes and give fleeting, frequent kisses all over the face and mouth. This kiss is recommended just before penetration and can be repeated during intercourse.

Tantric touches

The way you touch your lover during foreplay is often instinctive, but having a few tantric techniques to hand can lead to both of you experiencing new sensations.

Piercing It sounds alarming, but 'piercing' isn't about sticking needles in each other. Piercing means any gentle brushing of the skin with tender, dry feathery strokes. It can specifically refer to when the man brushes the woman's clit lightly with the base of his penis, a fabulous tantric technique that will have her begging for more.

Peacock's foot and tiger's nail This is the tradition of pressing or scratching the body with fingernails as a sign of intense passion. One of the main areas for doing this

was the woman's breast, although any erogenous zone will do. A curved line drawn with one nail is known as 'tiger's nail', while five crescent moons of nail digs is a 'peacock's foot'. Not everyone is comfortable with this kind of passionate clawing, so check with your lover first.

The biting of a boar and the broken cloud

Love bites are another intense form of stimulation that suit some couples and one the Kama Sutra recommends as a prelude to full sex. Gently nibbling your lover's skin to make a faint circle is called the broken cloud. If the mark is on the shoulder, where the thin skin is super-sensitive, it's known as the biting of a boar.

Lay your hands on me

Now that you've spent time meditating, kissing and caressing, you can move onto the more intimate ways of touching each other. The Kama Sutra recommended mutual masturbation before sex to ensure that both the man and woman were ready to enjoy the positions to the full.

How to touch a woman

❀ Never forget about yoni worship: compliment and talk to her for as long as you're touching her.

❀ Use lube and don't be offended if she doesn't get very wet very quickly. Many women take a few minutes to self-lubricate and some factors, such as medication or dehydration, can stop her lubricating altogether.

❀ Slow and steady is the key to stimulating her clit. When she says 'don't stop', don't stop!

❀ Rest your wrist on her pubic bone so your hand doesn't get tired and you can keep up the steady rhythm she needs.

❀ Experiment with different positions to see which one gets her the most aroused: kneeling between her legs or reaching around from behind while you're lying down can both be very effective.

❀ Don't shove your fingers inside her straight away. Bear in mind Vatsyayana's edict that women need 'tender beginnings'. She's more likely to get wet (or reach orgasm) through clitoral stimulation than if you use your fingers as a miniature penis.

- If you do place your fingers inside her, check she's wet enough for it to be comfortable. Gently bend your forefinger forward and 'beckon' the front wall of her vagina. This will stimulate her G-spot.
- Tease her by circling her clitoris with thumb and forefinger so it's already aroused when you touch it directly.

How to touch a man

- Don't forget the element of lingam worship. No man ever got sick of having a woman tell him how big his dick was.
- Ask him what he likes. Nothing else compares to communicating with your lover.
- Sit between his knees: that way you can touch him from an angle he can't manage himself, bringing novelty to an activity he has done every which way himself.
- Nestle his penis between your breasts for a soft, sensual caress that also gives your wrist time to rest.
- Lube, lube lube: he doesn't produce any natural lubrication so dry hands on the dry penis will cause friction burns – not what you want. Warm the lube between your palms before applying it.
- Make a loose fist with one hand and slide it all the way up the shaft of his penis. Think of it as the monarch's 'royal wave', only upside-down – and with a big cock in your hand. The twist stimulates the sensitive head. Meanwhile, your other hand is at the base of his penis, ready to work its way up and start the whole process again.

Oral sex

The Kama Sutra rates oral sex as the best way for lovers to prepare for intercourse, and has detailed instructions on techniques. While they are great as a guide, it's also important that you keep communicating with each other, and let each other know the moves that work the best.

Vatsyayana describes oral sex as an advanced foreplay technique, but these moves are so delicious there's nothing to stop you enjoying them in their own right, and using your mouths to bring each other to orgasm.

It's not always possible to focus on your deep breathing while you're giving oral sex, but you can inhale and exhale deeply while receiving your lover's lips.

Yoni kiss – how to give a woman oral sex

In Eastern cultures, the yoni symbolises reverence and respect for the woman as the giver of life. The yoni is the flowering lotus, with the clitoris as its bud. Kissing and caressing this delicate blossom releases sexual energy. The juices that flow when she's aroused also carry this energy. Oh, and licking and caressing the clitoris is also the most sure-fire route to getting a woman wet and ready for sex, or to make her come.

Pressing yoni kiss He presses lips against her vulva, using his hands on her thighs.

Outer yoni tongue strokes He gently spreads her pussy with his fingers and brushes her outer labia with his lips and tongue.

Inner yoni tongue strokes He explores a little deeper, brushing her inner labia and tasting her yoni juice.

Kissing the yoni blosssom He tenderly spreads his partner's labia to expose her clitoris. He gently strokes upward along the shaft and across the head of her clitoris with his tongue and licks up and down each side.

Butterfly flutter He softly flutters the top of the tongue over her clitoris. This move does more to drive a woman wild than any other in the Kama Sutra.

Sucking the yoni blossom He takes her clitoris in his mouth in a tender, sucking motion.

Kiss of the penetrating tongue As she gets more turned on, he uses his tongue as a mini penis, penetrating and withdrawing again.

Tantric tips for her pleasure
❀ Start by kissing her on the mouth – practising the mouth kisses you are about to apply to the yoni. Many ancient Indians believed the upper lip was linked to the clitoris, so this will prime her for your oral attentions.

- ❁ Worship her yoni: tell her you love the way she smells and tastes.
- ❁ The best position is with her lying or sitting on a bed with her thighs falling to either side. Placing a pillow under her hips will make it easier for you to see, feel and worship her yoni.
- ❁ Don't feel the need to move on from one of these techniques if she's enjoying it.
- ❁ If you think she's going to come, keep repeating the exact technique that got her to that point. Unlike men, women don't have that 'point of no return' when orgasm is inevitable. She needs the same delicious sensations right up until the moment her orgasm ripples through her body.

The lingam kiss – how to give a man oral sex

In the Kama Sutra, fellatio is called the lingam kiss, mouth congress or sucking a mango. It's intensely arousing for a man, and, with a little practice and care, easy for a woman to master. The Kama Sutra recommends the following seven techniques done in the right sequence.

Nimita Hold the base of his erection within your hand and ease it between your lips.

Parshvatodashta Cover the end of the penis with your fingers collected together like a flowerbud, then press the sides with your lips.

Bahih-Sandamsha Put the penis further into your mouth, then slowly withdraw it.

Chumbitaka Hold the penis in your hand, kiss it as though it were his lips.

Parimrishtaka Run your tongue all over the penis, paying particular attention to the tip.

Amrachushitaka Put it halfway into your mouth. Suck firmly (this is where the 'sucking a mango' name comes from).

Samgara Put the whole penis into your mouth and try to swallow it. Ease it gently towards the back of your throat to stop you gagging.

Tantric tips for his pleasure Don't forget to worship his lingam. Make mm-mmm noises and eye contact that show him how much you're enjoying this.

❀ Go with what feels good. The seven techniques are only a guide: if one of you hates/loves a certain move, then remove or repeat it until you see results.

❀ Keep one hand at the base of his penis. Not only does your enclosed fingers provide the sense of deeper penetration for him, it means you can control his thrusting and stop him gagging you.

❀ If you think he's about to come, press gently on his perineum. This will trip him over the edge into a deep, intense orgasm.

❀ The lingam kiss can be enjoyed in its own right as well as a part of foreplay. If you're going to bring him to a climax, agree before you begin whether you'll swallow his come. The Kama Sutra describes semen as precious juice, not to be spilled, and many men love to see their lover drink their juices. But if you don't like it, he must respect your wishes.

part two

the kama sutra positions

Welcome to the pages you've all been waiting for – the list of positions that have made the Kama Sutra famous all over the world. The Kama Sutra caters for all lovers, from the novice to the experienced, and we've indicated which positions are suitable for which moods and levels of physical ability.

The Kama Sutra positions

We've placed the poses in three categories, beginning with soft, sensual sex, working up through some more intense, energised moves and finishing with the most physically demanding poses.

 Level 1 Slow and Sensual – easy-to-do positions that everyone can do. Ideal for first-time tantra.

 Level 2 Deep and Dirty – for nights when passion takes you over and you need more thrusting.

 Level 3 Acrobatic Erotica – not for the faint-hearted. A flexible, strong body and a sense of humour are essential!

They can be done in no particular order, or in a sequence, starting with a soft, Level 1 pose and working up through Levels 2 and 3 as the heat between your bodies intensified. Likewise, if sex in a Level 3 position has worn you out, you might like to switch to a 1 or 2 to recharge your energy.

For each position, we've given you step-by-step instructions, tips on how to make sex more spiritual and, of course, the knowledge you need to chase the ultimate orgasm. And because we know how much you love to experiment, we've added a deliciously kinky, 21st-century twist to each position – a modern twist on a classic move.

Golden rules for Kama Sutra sex

The Kama Sutra teaches that the mind and spirit are the most powerful tools in your sexual repertoire, so before attempting these positions, lie side by side and synchronise your breathing (see page 34). Try to empty your minds of all thoughts but those of your lover: focus on a favourite body part or on your lover's face at the moment of climax.

Now look into your partner's eyes. Breathe in for four heartbeats and out for four heartbeats. Focusing on heartbeats instead of seconds means you are listening to the rhythms of your bodies. Hold that breath for two heartbeats, visualising the energy and life force – prana – and love that is flowing between the two of you. Exhale evenly for four heartbeats. Repeat even as you kiss and begin to make love.

Because you're not used to thinking about your breathing during sex, it can be easy to lose concentration. In fact, most of us find that as we near orgasm, our breathing becomes sharp and shallow. If one of you feels yourself slipping, stop what you're doing and focus on breathing for as long as it takes to get back in synch.

All these positions are designed around tantric breathing, and they'll be so much more orgasmic if you inhale and exhale in unison even during intercourse. Some Tantra devotees swear it can make orgasms last for an extra couple of seconds.

The Lotus

How to do it The Lotus is a classic sitting position from yoga. It lends itself beautifully to this intimate embrace. The lovers sit facing one another on a bed or mat, gazing at each other's faces and bodies to build up excitement. He sits with his legs crossed at the ankle, displaying his penis and uses his hand to make himself hard. She then shifts towards her lover and sits astride him, wrapping her arms and legs around his back. Instead of thrusting up and down, the woman clenches and unclenches her vaginal muscles, keeping up just enough pelvic movement to keep his penis erect, but not so much that he feels he's approaching climax.

Great for...
Slow intimacy and experimenting for couples new to tantric sex. The face-to-face contact means you can talk and giggle while you try your new techniques. The tenderness and honesty in this position mean that, emotionally, there's nowhere to hide.

Tantric tip
Tantric practitioners believe that if a man's spine is erect during intercourse, he's able to moderate his passion and delay his ejaculation for up to six hours. It's true that he's unlikely to climax too soon, and this is a fabulous position for letting him focus on his partner's pleasure.

21st-century twist
Take advantage of sex-toy technology to enhance your orgasms. Slipping a vibrating cock ring over the base of his penis will tease and tickle her clit, meaning she's more likely to climax than by penetration alone.

Milk and Water Embrace

How to do it When a man and a woman are very much in love with each other, and embrace as if they were entering each other's bodies, then it is called an embrace like a 'mixture of milk and water'. This position begins with a loving embrace that builds up intimacy and warmth.

On a chair on which the man can sit comfortably, with cushions if necessary, the woman sits astride his lap, facing away from him. He wraps her in his arms and plays with her clitoris. She guides his fingers and shows him what she wants. His penis rests between her buttocks, and she clenches her cheeks to tease him, loving how it feels as he gets harder. When she is wet with excitement, she lifts herself up ever so slightly and lowers herself onto him. Hold each other tightly: orgasm is achieved through rocking and thrusting. This can get quite tiring on her thighs, as she needs to raise and lower herself to control the depth and thrust of penetration.

. . . .

Tantric tip
The Milk and Water embrace starts off slowly but feels so delicious you might want to progress onto a more intense position, especially if she reaches orgasm first and he feels the need for more intense thrusting in order to come. If she gently bends over onto all fours and he kneels behind her, you can seamlessly slip into The Camel's Hump position (see page 80).

21st-century twist
Place a full-length mirror inches from your bed and watch yourselves move together as your bodies melt into one.

Great for...

As in all rear-entry sex, his penis is in prime position to stimulate her G-spot. And because there isn't a great range of movement, he's likely to last longer than usual – and the longer his dick strokes her G-spot, the more likely she is to come that way.

Great for...
The shallow penetration is great if he's got an oversized penis or she sometimes finds penetration uncomfortable.

The Twining

How to do it This is one of the first positions named in the Kama Sutra and perfect for beginners as it quickly builds up intimacy and arousal, and allows full body contact in a restful pose for both partners. Lie on your sides, facing one another. Look deep into each other's eyes and let your limbs entwine. Savour the sensuousness of your entangled bodies. She parts her legs slightly, allowing him access to her vagina, and he penetrates her. Placing her upper thigh across her lover, the woman can increase intensity and depth. She can alter the clasp's tightness by raising or lowering her leg. If you want a bit more in-out, he can raise himself up on his knee while she remains on her side with one leg slung over his thigh.

65

Tantric tip
This is really intimate and you can speak and kiss throughout: in fact, the success of the position depends on you remaining entwined (hence the name), otherwise gravity intervenes and you'll fall back onto the other side of the bed. A Kama Sutra kiss is perfect for this position: try the upper lip kiss (see page 39) to infuse her clitoris with extra sexual energy.

21st-century twist
Cover yourselves in massage oil or lube and slip-slide all over a rubber sheet to add a challenge and element of fun to this position.

The Elephant Posture

How to do it She lies face down with breasts, stomach, thighs and feet all touching the bed. He lies over her with the small of his back arched inwards. She raises her buttocks so that he can penetrate her – she might find it easier to slip a pillow under her hips so that her ass is pointing upwards and he has a good view of her vagina when she spreads her legs. Once he is inside her, she can intensify the sensations for both partners by pressing her thighs closely together.

Great for...
This is great for the man who likes to be in control. Penetration stimulates her G-spot. She can barely move because of the weight of her lover. Many women find this lack of control incredibly arousing.

Tantric tip
This was inspired by the mating patterns of the elephants in India, which isn't the most obviously erotic image for modern lovers – however, the thrill of this position is timeless. Unleash your own inner wild animal and howl as loudly and passionately as you both can.

21st-century twist
This is great for a little light spanking, which as well as being a naughty thrill, also gets blood flowing to the whole pelvic region, making it even more sensitive. A light slap to the thigh with the back of a hand or a spanking paddle here can take sex in the Elephant Posture to a new dimension.

The Yawning

How to do it She lies back on the bed and spreads her legs wide – which is where this position gets its name. He can give her oral sex or play with her clitoris until she's begging to have him inside her, then props himself up on his forearms and enters her. Keeping her thighs open, she can then experiment with different leg positions such as extending them or crossing her ankles behind his back. Each time she moves her legs, the angle of her vagina changes slightly and penetration feels different. Each couple will have a favourite version of this pose – it's fun to make up as many as you can until you find one that works for both of you.

Great for...
Deep penetration and clit stim in one: she can push her pelvis forward and furiously rub her clitoris on the base of his pubic bone to create the friction she needs to reach a climax.

Tantric tip
The Kama Sutra says that in this position the woman 'puts aside all bashfulness'. Both abandon any shyness and be vocal and explicit about the delicious sensations you're making each other feel.

21st-century twist
Deprive yourselves of your primary senses and rely on touch, taste and smell to experience this position in its fullest intensity. Wear earplugs and turn out the light – you explore each other's bodies in a completely different way as you rely on hands and mouths alone to guide you.

The Dominant Goddess

How to do it In Hindu belief, every god has his corresponding goddess to give him energy and strength. The literature often mentions goddesses on top of their gods in sexual union – a position replicated here. He lies on his back, while she straddles his body before gently sliding down onto his erection and using her thighs to move up and down, with her whole body rocking back and forth as far as she is able.

She can lean back to increase the angle of his penetration, but this must be done sloooooooowly as his penis might not be used to bending at that angle. If he makes a whimper that sounds more like pain than pleasure, stick to the straight-up version of this posture. If he gets frustrated at not being able to control the thrusting, then he can guide her waist and buttocks to bounce her up and down.

- -

Great for...
This is an ideal position during pregnancy as her bump won't be squashed. He has easy access to her clitoris and can stroke and tease her to orgasm with little effort, especially if he uses a vibrator.

Tantric tip
As she straddles him, both imagine that she is a life-giving goddess and breathe in time, feeling the raw sexual energy pulse between your bodies.

21st-century twist
Ancient Indians used to adorn the body and you can do the same – from flirty peephole bras at the tame end of the scale, to nipple clamps at the hardcore end. This makes his view even more thrilling, and can intensify her sensations and orgasm.

The Pressing Position

How to do it He kneels on the bed and she lies back and brings her knees up to her chin, so that when he enters her, her feet are at either side of his head or resting on his chest. He holds onto her thighs or shins, and she grabs onto his hips. She lies back and raises both her feet on his chest and her knees to her shoulders. He should take care when penetrating her, as the vagina is shortened and the sensation is intense.

The woman needs to be bold and tell her partner just what she likes and how far he can thrust without causing pain. Using her feet, she can steady him and stop him banging too hard. She can move her hips from side to side while he holds her ankles or thighs to help increase her grip on him. In a break from thrusting, the man can pay attention to her feet. Holding a foot in each hand, he can massage them.

Great for...
Deep penetration at an unusual angle. She can reach underneath and tug his balls or stroke his perineum to intensify his orgasm.

Tantric tip
If she raises her right leg up to the top of his chest, she will be able to feel his heartbeat with the sole of her foot – an incredibly tender and bonding experience.

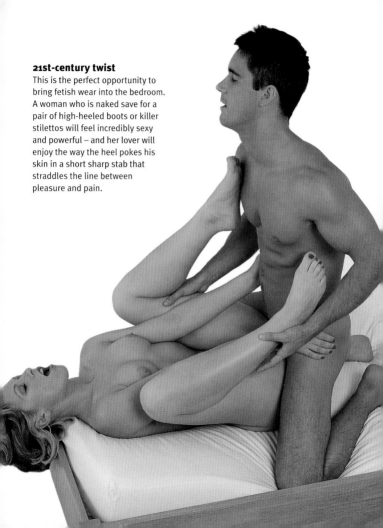

21st-century twist

This is the perfect opportunity to bring fetish wear into the bedroom. A woman who is naked save for a pair of high-heeled boots or killer stilettos will feel incredibly sexy and powerful – and her lover will enjoy the way the heel pokes his skin in a short sharp stab that straddles the line between pleasure and pain.

The Second Position of the Perfumed Garden

How to do it Begin as with the Yawning (see page 65) but instead of lying with her legs on the bed, she bends them back so that her knees are touching her chest and her legs are outstretched, slightly parted so he can bend down and kiss her. He needs to use his hands to support his weight: she can grip her ankles to steady her legs and allow him to enter her more easily.

Great for...
The Kama Sutra recommends this for a man with a very short penis as this allows the deepest penetration of all. She may find vaginal thrusting too painful and stimulating – especially if his penis is larger than usual – and need him to back off a little.

Tantric tip
This position really stretches the backs of her legs. To warm up spiritually, you might want to attend a yoga class or watch a yoga DVD together before making love.

21st-century twist
Introduce an element of fantasy by assuming the roles of sexy servant and dominant master. She wears tie-side panties that he has to tear off or push to one side before he can penetrate her.

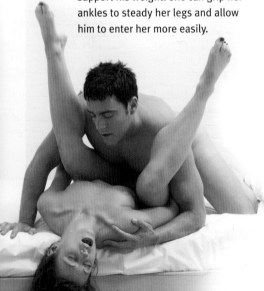

Congress of a Cow – woman on top

How to do it This is the most common position for giving each other oral sex at the same time – often known as the '69'. He lies flat on his back with his arms by his sides or around her buttocks. She's on all fours with her bottom in the air, hovering over his face. She rests on her forearms, her mouth poised over his penis. The benefits of this position are that she can control the rhythm of the cunnilingus she's receiving by rocking her hips in time. Her breasts will brush against his belly and thighs, which will turn him on and the friction on her nipples will stimulate her, too.

Great for...
This is a real treat for the guy. He gets all the pleasure with half the work! His arms are free to caress her or to stimulate himself if she gets tired.

Tantric tip
It's not easy to both give and receive oral sex at the same time, so don't worry if you don't see stars the first time you do it. Because it's hard to concentrate on giving head and getting it at the same time, take it in turns – perfectly in keeping with the Kama Sutra spirit of selfless loving. Spend alternate minutes stimulating one another's genitals – this should build up to a tremendous orgasm for both of you.

21st-century twist
Sucking on each others' toes requires impeccable foot hygiene but it's a surprisingly overwhelming feeling – just the soft sensation you need during this physically demanding position.

Congress of a Cow
– man on top

How to do it She lies back on the bed, legs slightly parted, arms by her side. He crouches over her on all fours and is in an excellent position to play with her breasts. This is a comfortable position for him because his neck won't start to ache. He can also use her inner thighs as a pillow. He can see exactly what he's doing so there's no excuse for him not finding her clitoris and paying it lots of attention with his tongue.

72

Great for...

Guys with oversized penises and women who are overwhelmed when giving oral sex. It's not easy for her to take him fully into her mouth, but he can thrust against her neck, cheeks and breasts and she can use her tongue on his anus, balls and perineum (the sensitive skin between his balls and anus).

Tantric tip

Again, it's tricky to do two things at once, three if you count your tantric breathing. This is perfect for those times when you're feeling fun and frisky and orgasm isn't the immediate goal. Use it as foreplay and savour what you've just done while you're making love in a more conventional position.

21st-century twist

Slather flavoured lubes or chocolate body paint all over the front of your bodies before you begin. Use your mouths to lick as much sexy juice as you can off your partner, ensuring that every erogenous zone gets a delicious tongue bath.

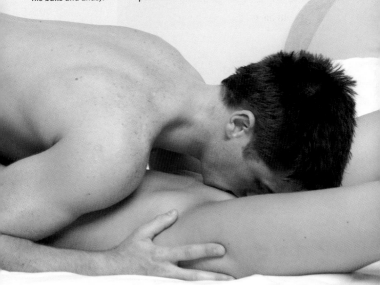

The Widely Opened Position

How to do it Begin as though you were making love in the missionary position: he's on top, resting on his elbows, she's lying on her back. Once he's snugly inside her, she wraps her legs around his back, raising her pelvis as she does so, ensuring that her clitoris remains in contact with his pubic bone. He then rises up on all fours, so that he is bearing her whole body weight with his back and shoulders. He stays absolutely stationary while she rubs her clitoris against his pubic bone, making sure she gets the stimulation she needs to orgasm, which gives him just enough friction to maintain his erection, but not quite enough to cause him to climax. As she approaches orgasm, she can afford to arouse him a little more. If she pulls herself only halfway onto his penis, she focuses on the nerve endings in the super-sensitive tip of his penis.

. . . .

Tantric tip
With so much to do, it's easy to lose track of the breathing that is so vital to Kama Sutra sex. To help you synchronise your breath, buy a CD of gentle ambient music from your local new-age shop and use the soft pulsing beat of the music as a guide.

Great for...

This position is fabulous for achieving simultaneous orgasm. Men usually come sooner than women, so anything that speeds up her climax and slows his down will up the odds of you coming at the same time. This position gives her clitoris full exposure to the friction of intercourse and she controls that friction, meaning she can rub at a pace and intensity that suits her perfectly. But his climax is delayed: the effort it takes him to carry her can buy precious extra minutes of intercourse as blood rushes away from his erection to his upper body muscles.

21st-century twist

The Widely Opened Position obviously depends on a reasonably light woman and a reasonably strong man who doesn't have any back problems. If this is too much, pile cushions in your boudoir or invest in some sex furniture – specially designed pieces to accommodate and support two ambitious lovers.

The Turning Position

How to do it Think of it as the missionary position, but the man has spun round: that's where it gets its name from. The very ambitious might be tempted to start off in male missionary position and then turn round like a corkscrew, but I would advise against this for all but the most advanced Tantra practitioners. Instead, she lies on her back with her legs slightly apart, while he lies on top of her, facing her feet. His torso is between her legs while his arms are either side of her legs and his legs either side of her shoulders. Penetration is almost impossible unless she tilts her pelvis upwards to accommodate his penis: if she puts a couple of pillows underneath her hips it will be much easier. The shallow depth means that you use a gentle rocking motion rather than the vigorous thrusting you can get away with in other positions.

76

Great for...

He can't penetrate her very deeply, so the ultra-sensitive tip of his penis gets lots of attention. She will enjoy the feeling of his balls caressing her vagina.

Tantric tip

It's hard to keep the synchronised breathing and eye contact that makes Kama Sutra sex so special when your heads are at opposite ends of the bed. Hold onto each other's feet, and press the soft fleshy centres of each other's toes. This is an ancient yoga move that will help the energy flow between you and keep you connected.

21st-century twist

This is great for trying female domination – one sharp move from her, and his penis will be in agony. So manipulate that fact. Rent a dominatrix outfit and brandish a whip – she can even place the whip across his raised arms to make his surrender complete.

The Yab-Yum

How to do it The Yab-Yum is a more demanding version of the Lotus (see page 59), offering the same degree of intimacy but deeper penetration. He sits on the bed with his legs bent: she wraps her arms and legs around him and lowers herself onto his erection. Once he's snug inside her, she slowly raises her legs over his shoulders. This offers her the deeper penetration she needs, while the top of her vagina is stretched and lengthened by this position, denying him the stimulation at the tip of the penis that might trip him over into premature climax. He can pop his hands, or a pillow, under her ass so she is slightly lifted, which makes for better clitoral stimulation on the base of his pubic bone. He thrusts gently while she squeezes her PC muscles (see page 25) to massage him to orgasm.

78

. . . .

Great for...
Women who love deep penetration but don't want to have rear-entry sex. The top of her vagina is stretched and lengthened by this position, denying him the stimulation at the tip of the penis that might trip him over into premature climax.

Tantric tip
When you've both reached orgasm, don't pull apart: satisfied, remain in the Yab-Yum position, breathing harmoniously until his penis is totally limp. We rarely allow this to happen, but it's a very gentle, intimate end to a lovemaking session.

21st-century twist
Hooking her ankles together with a pair of leg irons introduces an element of kinky bondage, which juxtaposes well with the tenderness of the Yab-Yum. If you do this, she'll need to fasten the irons or cuffs around her ankles before she lifts them over his head.

The Camel's Hump

How to do it He needs a full erection. She stands leaning against a wall or holding onto something like a windowsill or bed-end for support. He gets behind her and bends his legs until he's low enough to penetrate her from the rear. Both bend your legs until you've found a position you're both comfortable with, and gently bounce your way to a climax. This one takes some getting used to, so if she finds it hard to balance, she can bend over until she's confident enough to stand up. If there's a discrepancy in height, she could stand on a step or the edge of a bed.

80

Great for...

This is the perfect position if she's got very long, lean legs or she's the taller partner. It's ideal for an elephant woman and a hare man, as her legs act as an extension of the vagina, making for tighter penetration for him and stimulating the nerve endings on her labia and inner thighs.

21st-century twist

This is also a great position for couples who enjoy watching pornography together. Think of it as safe group sex: with the right erotic movie and a carefully positioned television screen, you can both enjoy the stimulus of watching other bodies while enjoying the sensation of your lover's, safe in the knowledge your steamy little secret stays between the two of you.

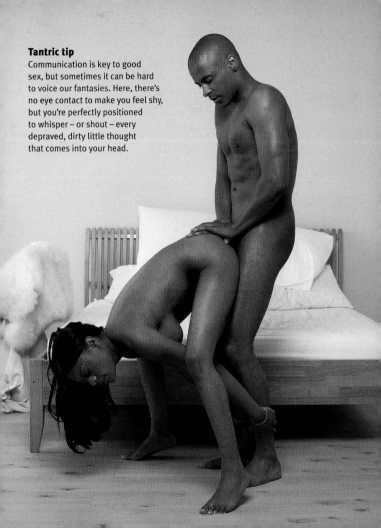

Tantric tip

Communication is key to good sex, but sometimes it can be hard to voice our fantasies. Here, there's no eye contact to make you feel shy, but you're perfectly positioned to whisper – or shout – every depraved, dirty little thought that comes into your head.

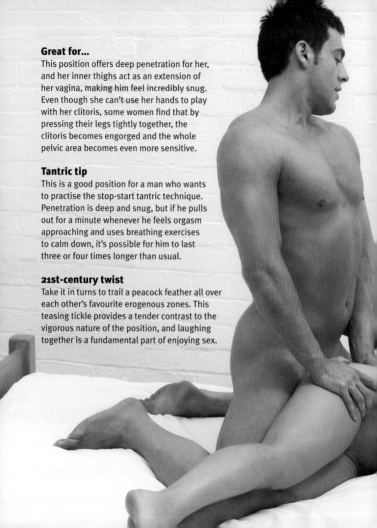

Great for...

This position offers deep penetration for her, and her inner thighs act as an extension of her vagina, making him feel incredibly snug. Even though she can't use her hands to play with her clitoris, some women find that by pressing their legs tightly together, the clitoris becomes engorged and the whole pelvic area becomes even more sensitive.

Tantric tip

This is a good position for a man who wants to practise the stop-start tantric technique. Penetration is deep and snug, but if he pulls out for a minute whenever he feels orgasm approaching and uses breathing exercises to calm down, it's possible for him to last three or four times longer than usual.

21st-century twist

Take it in turns to trail a peacock feather all over each other's favourite erogenous zones. This teasing tickle provides a tender contrast to the vigorous nature of the position, and laughing together is a fundamental part of enjoying sex.

The Side Clasp

How to do it She lies on her side with her legs at a ninety-degree angle to her torso, so that from above her body forms an L-shape. He kneels on the bed, his hips aligned with hers. If he wants to, he can put his hands on her hips to steady himself. She parts her legs slightly to allow him to penetrate, and then squeezes them together to give his penis a delicious massage as he thrusts in and out of her. She can twist her upper body so that she's lying on her back, but keeps her legs to one side – this way you combine the snug, rear-entry physical sensations of this position with face-to-face contact.

83

The Sporting of the Swan

How to do it He lies flat on his back. Facing away from him, she squats over him, facing his feet, and slowly lowers herself onto his erection, tucking her feet in close to his upper thighs. She leans on her hands and bounces up and down and rolls her hips in a gentle figure-of-eight movement to stimulate him. Flexible women can lean back so that their backs are resting on their lover's chest, which will increase the tightness of penetration. Take care when leaning forward in this position, as it forces his erection into an unusual, and potentially uncomfortable, position.

Great for...

It's empowering for women and many find it the best way to reach orgasm during sex as she controls the rhythm and depth of penetration – and access to her own clitoris means she can get herself off with her own fingers. It's also a relaxing, low-energy position for men who usually take the lead in bed.

Tantric tip

You can't see each other in this position, so it's important that you use breathwork to stay connected. Try breathing in for four beats, holding your breath for two and then out again for four. As well as synchronising your bodies and souls, the tension and release of the held breath mimics orgasm – and primes your body for an amazing climax.

21st-century twist

Experiment with butt plugs. These sex toys are designed to pop in the anus and often have decorative or kitsch attachments like fake ponytails. For her, they'll increase the satisfied, full-up feeling of penetration in her vagina, and for him, they'll stimulate the prostate gland, giving him an out-of-this-world orgasm. Lube up and gently insert them into each other's asses before sex.

Suspended Congress

How to do it He begins on his knees and asks her to lower herself onto his erection, facing him. As she does, she wraps her legs around his waist and puts her arms up around his neck. Then he slowly stands up, so that he's holding her in his arms and slowly rocks and bounces her to a climax. The Kama Sutra states that this position is to be sustained for minutes on end without any support, but that's hardly realistic, so he might want to sit her on the edge of a bed, chair, table or worktop – any nearby surface that's roughly the height of his pelvis.

Great for...

This position shows off a strong male body and brute strength, and makes the woman feel classically feminine and vulnerable. Although neither of them have their hands free to stimulate her clitoris, the friction of her clitoris grinding against his pubic bone should get her off.

Tantric tip

Try this position in a private pool scattered with lotus flowers next time you're on holiday. Your muscles will be supported by the water: you can then concentrate on the sensations you're feeling rather than using strength to support each other.

21st-century twist

If she is blindfolded in this position, her feelings of vulnerability and trust will be completely overwhelming, he needs to keep his eyes open – he doesn't want to drop his precious load!

Riding the Horse

How to do it He lies on his back with his knees curled up to his chest. She is in control and will find his facial expressions a big turn-on as she slowly begins to masturbate him. She straddles him with his legs under her arms to steady her, and her legs either side of his body. She lowers herself until he's deep inside her and moves up and down in a pumping action, controlling the depth and motion of the thrusts.

Great for...
This is the classic goddess worship position – the woman here is powerful. He should praise her face, breasts and pussy using explicit language that gets both partners hot and steamy.

Tantric tip
Although the actual position is quite physically demanding, the rate at which you do it is variable so you can alter it depending on your mood. You both get a great view and this position allows his penis to explore every inch of the sensitive walls of her vagina.

21st-century twist
As both of you are so busy balancing, your all-important clitoral stimulation might get bypassed, take the hands-free option with a tiny clitoral vibrator. Trail it over your bodies before squeezing it between her clit and his pubic bone.

The Cats

How to do it She begins on all fours either on the floor or a bed. He carefully takes hold of her ankles and raises them level with his hips, so her hands are the only part of her body on the floor and her pelvis is in mid air. The man lifts her legs up and holds them spread apart as he penetrates her from behind. She can also wrap her legs around the man's waist crossing her ankles behind his back for extra support. He enters her slowly (depending on your bodies, it may be a good idea for him to bend his knees a bit). He gets a great view of her ass as he drives his dick into her. Her nipples have got lots of blood flow, which means the whole front of her body will be sensitive if you get tired and decide to then switch to a face-to-face position. However, she will need good upper body strength to support herself in this position for any length of time: resting on the edge of a bed will take the strain off her arms and wrists.

Great for...

It's great for a hare man and an elephant woman as penetration is very snug here. Even the smallest penis or the loosest pussy will achieve a happy partnership in this position!

Tantric tip

In this pose, the man is completely in control, like a strong tom cat. It's great for outdoor sex when you both want to get back to nature. The ancient Indians would have made love under the stars. Isn't it time you tried the same thing?

21st-century twist

Before making love in this position, why not invest in collars and leads and take it in turn to lead each other around the house? Experimenting with control and surrender like this is a fun game that can tap into your deepest, darkest fantasies.

Great for...

Showing off! This is one of the most demanding positions in the Kama Sutra, and suited to yoga practitioners as the woman needs to be supple and agile. The man also needs to be confident that he can support her weight.

The Hanging Bow

How to do it Vatsyayana describes the hanging bow as making the lovers look 'like links in a chain' and you're certainly tied together. Begin by standing opposite each other. He bends his knees until she can comfortably lower herself onto his erection. You begin by having standing-up sex, as in Suspended Congress (see page 86). When you've got the hang of that, he grabs her hips and leans back slightly, being sure to keep his balance. Letting go of his neck, clutching his forearms for support, she gradually leans backwards until she is able to let go and place her hands on the ground. Then she can raise her feet off the floor completely, clasping her ankles around his back for support, so you can rock rather than thrust. The posture completely changes the angle of penetration, shortening the vagina and pressing the penis down.

91

. . . .

Tantric tip

This pose demonstrates complete trust in each other's mobility. Hold that thought as you breathe in and out in time with each other.

21st-century twist

Because he is staring directly down at her pussy, increasing his visual pleasure is easy. Shaving or waxing all of her pubic hair and decorating her pubic mound with stick-on body jewels will send this already hot position right off the scale.

Kama's Wheel

How to do it He sits with his legs outstretched and parted. She faces him and lowers herself onto his penis, extending her legs over his so that they point out past his back. His arms encircle her, supporting her upper back and her hands grasp the outside of his upper arms. Both partners lean back, creating the circular shape that gives this position its name. Many women love the sense of surrender and vulnerability this position promotes: with her head flung back to expose her breasts and upper body, and her legs parted to reveal her clitoris and vulva, she can revel in the attention as her lover enjoys the view.

92

Great for...
Kama's Wheel promotes enormous feelings of intimacy and trust as you're both relying on each other to support your body weight. It's all about balance and equality, two qualities vital to tantric sex.

Tantric tip
This position was originally about meditation rather than orgasm and isn't always erotically satisfying. Thrusting is almost impossible in this position so he can't race towards a climax. It can be very liberating for a man to focus on intercourse when orgasm isn't the sole aim.

21st-century twist
Clitoral stimulation is unfortunately almost impossible without the aid of stimulation. Strap-on vibrators that rest lightly on the clit but still give him access to penetrate come into their own in positions like this. When she comes, the contractions could be enough to make him climax without thrusting.

The Rising

How to do it She lies on her back, her hands propping up her weight as though she's about to do a shoulder stand. He kneels before her and pulls her ankles up towards his shoulders, so her legs are resting on his body and her ankles are around his neck. The woman, enfolded within the man's thighs, raises her legs up high with her feet and ankles resting on his shoulders. She holds onto his hips while he clasps her ankles or thighs. He slowly moves his penis in her vagina using slow circular motions while she lies still and enjoys the feeling of him exploring her depths. It needs suppleness and stamina. If she's got neck or back problems, don't attempt this position.

94

Great for...
The Kama Sutra recommends this pose for the elephant-type woman as the vagina is much shortened in this pose, making penetration feel tighter: a smaller woman may be uncomfortable.

Tantric tip
Penetration feels a bit weird at first, so thrust slowly to begin with. Try a few shallow thrusts, where only the head of the penis enters the vagina, followed by a deeper one, and then the same in reverse. Time the thrusts with your breathing patterns.

21st-century twist
Make your own 'gonzo' film. Gonzo is the adult movie industry's word for a porn film shot by one of the participants. He can use a hand-held video camera or even a mobile phone to capture the unique view of her body this gives him – and her hands are free to return the favour.

Ann Summers

The ultimate girlie night in...

Host an Ann Summers Party, at home and amongst friends, and you'll get:

40% off any sex toy or lingerie set plus 10% of total sales at your party to spend on anything in the Ann Summers catalogue.

To book a party please call **0845 456 2599**

or go to www.annsummers.com/parties

Please quote reference PPM when booking to secure this exclusive discount.